GRAPHIC MYTHOLOGY
CHINESE MYTHS

by Rob Shone

illustrated by Claudia Saraceni

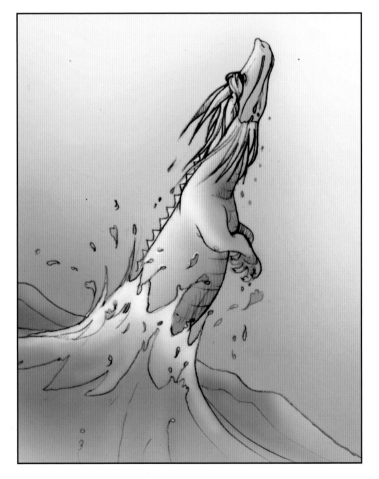

The Rosen Publishing Group, Inc., New York

Published in 2006 by The Rosen Publishing Group, Inc.
29 East 21st Street, New York, NY 10010
Copyright © 2006 David West Books

First edition, 2006

Designed and produced by
David West Books

Editors: Charlotte Cattermole, Kate Newport

Photo credits:
    Page 5 bottom, Ulrike Hammerlich/iStockphoto.com

Library of Congress Cataloging-in-Publication Data

Shone, Rob.
    Chinese myths / by Rob Shone; illustrated by Claudia Saraceni.
    p. cm. – (Graphic mythology)
    Includes index.
    ISBN 1-4042-0799-6 (library binding) – ISBN 1-4042-0811-9 (pbk.) – ISBN 1-4042-6251-2 (6 pack)
    1. Mythology, Chinese. I. Title. II. Series.

    BL1825.S56 2005
    299.5'1113--dc22

                                        2005017826

Manufactured in China

CONTENTS

TALES FROM CHINA

Chinese mythology is a term used to describe the varied folk tales and legends of China that have been passed down from generation to generation and that still influence Chinese society today. As with other cultures, there was a long tradition of oral storytelling before anything was written down.

Yin Yang is a symbol from Daoism. Yin is the dark color and is meant to be man and the moon. Yang is the light color and is woman and the sun. Yin and Yang could not grow and exist without each other.

MYTHS AND RELIGION

There are three main influences on Chinese culture. These are Confucianism, Daoism, and Buddhism. Confucianism values rationalism, and therefore Chinese written records are very factual. However, Daoism and Buddhism look at the world in a spiritual way. Daoism is about harmony with nature and balance in life. Buddhism teaches spiritual purity. All three helped to develop Chinese stories.

Ananda was Buddha's favorite apostle, as well as his cousin and friend. He helped to spread Buddhism, and eventually it came to China.

The Chinese have great respect for the tiger. It is considered to be the king of all the animals. There are many stories and myths about this great creature.

ANIMAL MAGIC

Animals are very important in Chinese mythology. In particular, there are four sacred animals. Three are mythical—the dragon, unicorn, and the phoenix—and the fourth is the tortoise. Many of the gods of Chinese tales have mixtures of animal and human features, and often possess the best, or worst, qualities of both.

FESTIVAL

There are many different celebrations that take place each year in China. These festivals honor the traditions and family histories of the Chinese people. The mid-autumn festival, for example, used to be the time when families made sacrifices to the moon goddess. Today, it celebrates the family.

Originally performed to please the dragon and to ask for water, the dragon dance is now popular entertainment at festivals.

THREE CHINESE MYTHS

Chinese myths have changed over time to fit in with current social values. However, the main themes, such as creation and religion, are still present.

THE FOUR DRAGONS

Characters from a Chinese animal myth, the four dragons watch over Earth and try to help humans. The story tells of how the four great Chinese rivers were created. It also explains why the dragon is so respected and worshipped in Chinese culture.

The Jade Emperor
As the ruler of heaven, the Jade Emperor, also known to children as Grandpa Heaven, is one of the most important gods. He also rules over life on Earth.

Dragons
In Chinese mythology, the dragon is a very powerful creature and is said to have been on Earth long before humans. They are generally described as good and kind to humans, unlike dragons in other cultures, who are often portrayed as wicked or destructive. In some tales, however, they do hurt humans. The dragon is also very important to Chinese society. It was even used as a symbol of power on the robes of emperors.

NU WA MAKES PEOPLE AND MENDS A HOLE IN THE SKY

Chinese myths have changed so many times over the years that there are now several different versions of many of them. The story of how Nu Wa made people to live on Earth is just one of the many creation myths from China.

Nu Wa

Nu Wa is the goddess who separated heaven from Earth. In doing so, she created China. She has the tail of a snake and the head and body of a human. She is also known as Mixi.

THE TEN SUNS

This is a cosmological myth, used to explain how the universe works. There is also a Mongolian version of it, called the Seven Suns. This particular tale is called the Ten Suns because the Chinese week has ten days. The ancient Chinese believed that there was a different sun for each day.

Yi
A great archer in Chinese mythology, Yi carries a magical bow and arrows. Yi is given a task by Di Jun that will help to save China.

Emperor Yao
A semi mythical figure, Emperor Yao is a kind and wise ruler who looks after his people.

Di Jun
The father of the Ten Suns, Di Jun must try to encourage his children to behave in a way that will keep the Earth safe.

THE FOUR DRAGONS

IN ANCIENT CHINA...

...THE CREATURE THAT WAS LOVED ABOVE ALL OTHER CREATURES...

...WAS THE DRAGON!

THERE WERE NO RIVERS, LAKES, OR EVEN STREAMS. ONLY THE SEA, THE HOME OF DRAGONS.

HIGH ABOVE THEIR OCEAN HOME, FOUR DRAGONS— YELLOW DRAGON, BLACK DRAGON, PEARL DRAGON, AND LONG DRAGON...

...WERE FLYING AMONG THE CLOUDS.

LISTEN! SOMEONE FAR BELOW IS CALLING OUT.

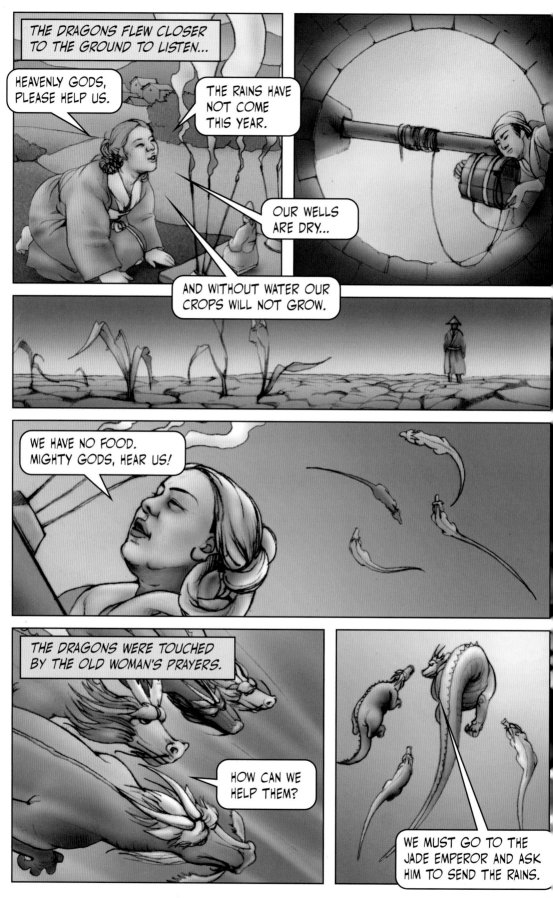

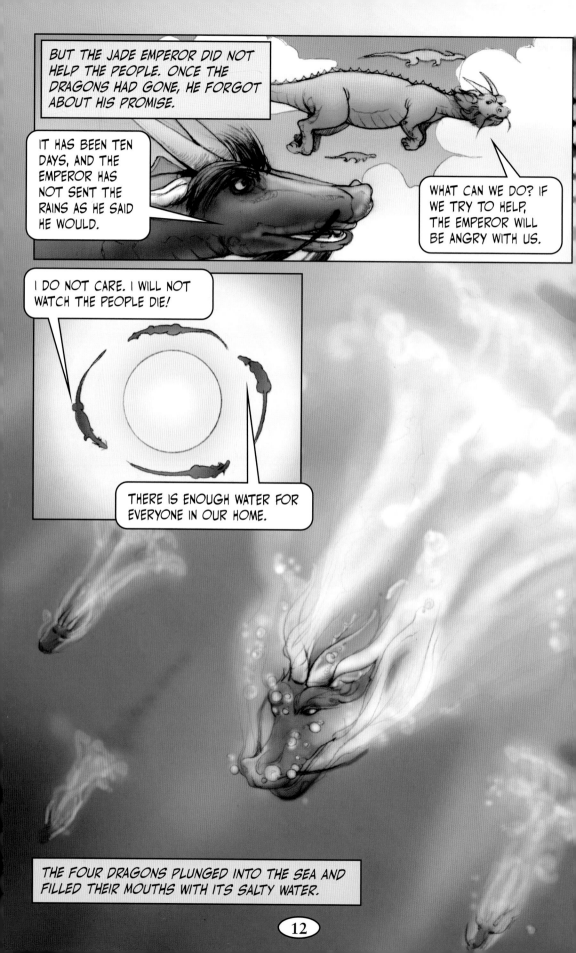

BUT THE JADE EMPEROR DID NOT HELP THE PEOPLE. ONCE THE DRAGONS HAD GONE, HE FORGOT ABOUT HIS PROMISE.

IT HAS BEEN TEN DAYS, AND THE EMPEROR HAS NOT SENT THE RAINS AS HE SAID HE WOULD.

WHAT CAN WE DO? IF WE TRY TO HELP, THE EMPEROR WILL BE ANGRY WITH US.

I DO NOT CARE. I WILL NOT WATCH THE PEOPLE DIE!

THERE IS ENOUGH WATER FOR EVERYONE IN OUR HOME.

THE FOUR DRAGONS PLUNGED INTO THE SEA AND FILLED THEIR MOUTHS WITH ITS SALTY WATER.

12

FROM THE SEA, THEY SOARED INTO THE SKY...

...AND OVER THE DRY LANDS.

THE WATER THAT SPILLED FROM THEIR MOUTHS TURNED INTO MIST.

THE MIST TURNED INTO CLOUDS.

AGAIN AND AGAIN, THE DRAGONS FLEW FROM THE SEA TO THE SKY AND BACK.

SOON, THIN WISPY CLOUDS CRISSCROSSED THE SKY.

WITH EACH JOURNEY, THE CLOUDS GREW, BECOMING THICKER AND THICKER...

...DARKER AND DARKER.

15

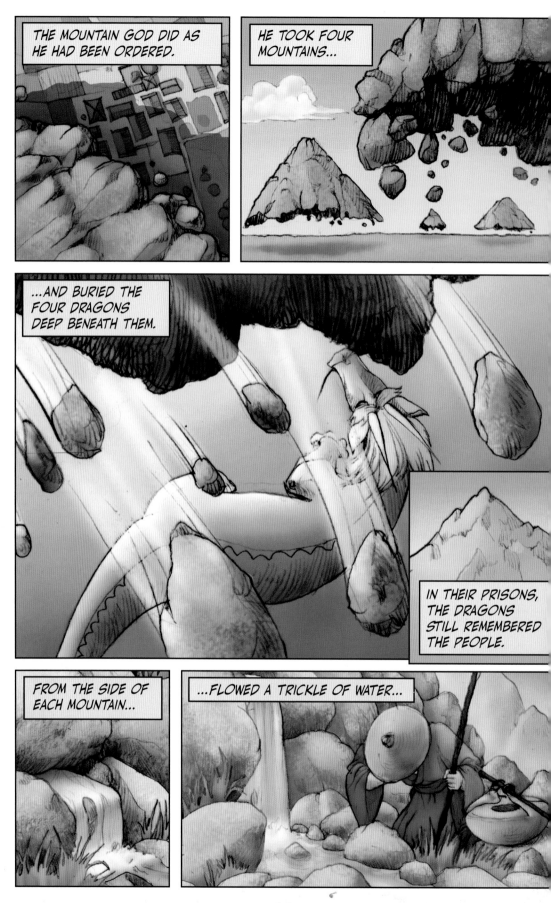

THE MOUNTAIN GOD DID AS HE HAD BEEN ORDERED.

HE TOOK FOUR MOUNTAINS...

...AND BURIED THE FOUR DRAGONS DEEP BENEATH THEM.

IN THEIR PRISONS, THE DRAGONS STILL REMEMBERED THE PEOPLE.

FROM THE SIDE OF EACH MOUNTAIN...

...FLOWED A TRICKLE OF WATER...

...THAT GREW

...AND GREW!

THE FOUR DRAGONS HAD BECOME CHINA'S FOUR GREAT RIVERS: THE YELLOW RIVER; THE PEARL RIVER; THE YANGTZE, OR LONG RIVER, AND THE HEILONGJIANG, OR BLACK RIVER.

PEOPLE WOULD NEVER BE THIRSTY AGAIN. AND ALTHOUGH THEY WERE NO LONGER DRAGONS, THE SPIRITS OF THE FOUR FRIENDS FINALLY REACHED THEIR HOME—THE SEA.

THE END

NU WA MAKES PEOPLE AND MENDS A HOLE IN THE SKY

BEFORE THERE WERE PEOPLE ON EARTH, THERE LIVED THE GODDESS NU WA.

NU WA WAS HALF WOMAN...

...AND HALF SERPENT.

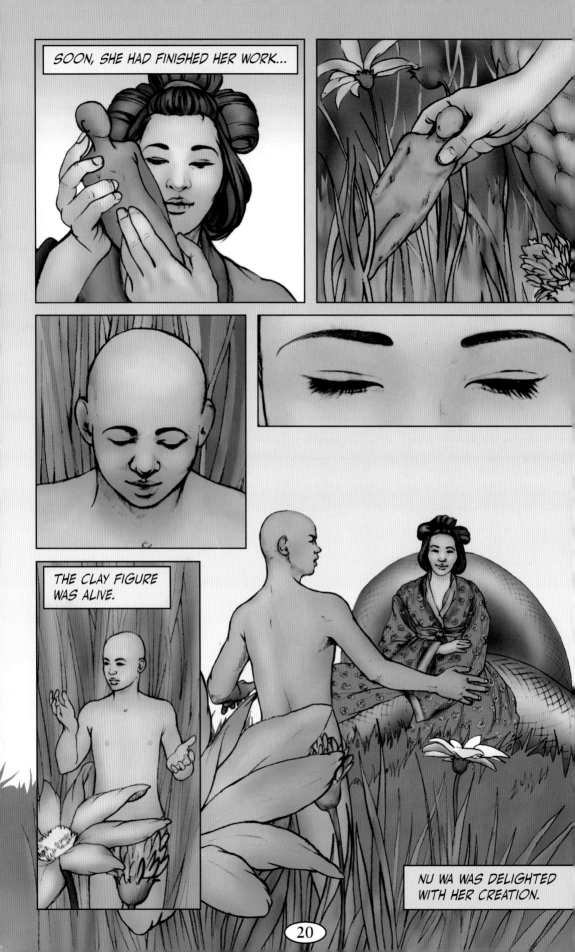

SOON, SHE HAD FINISHED HER WORK...

THE CLAY FIGURE WAS ALIVE.

NU WA WAS DELIGHTED WITH HER CREATION.

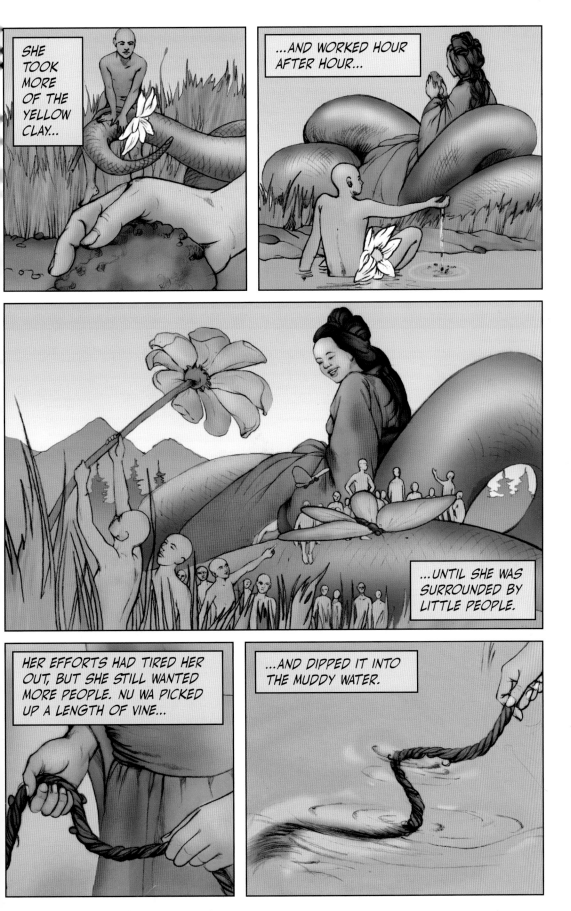

SHE TOOK MORE OF THE YELLOW CLAY...

...AND WORKED HOUR AFTER HOUR...

...UNTIL SHE WAS SURROUNDED BY LITTLE PEOPLE.

HER EFFORTS HAD TIRED HER OUT, BUT SHE STILL WANTED MORE PEOPLE. NU WA PICKED UP A LENGTH OF VINE...

...AND DIPPED IT INTO THE MUDDY WATER.

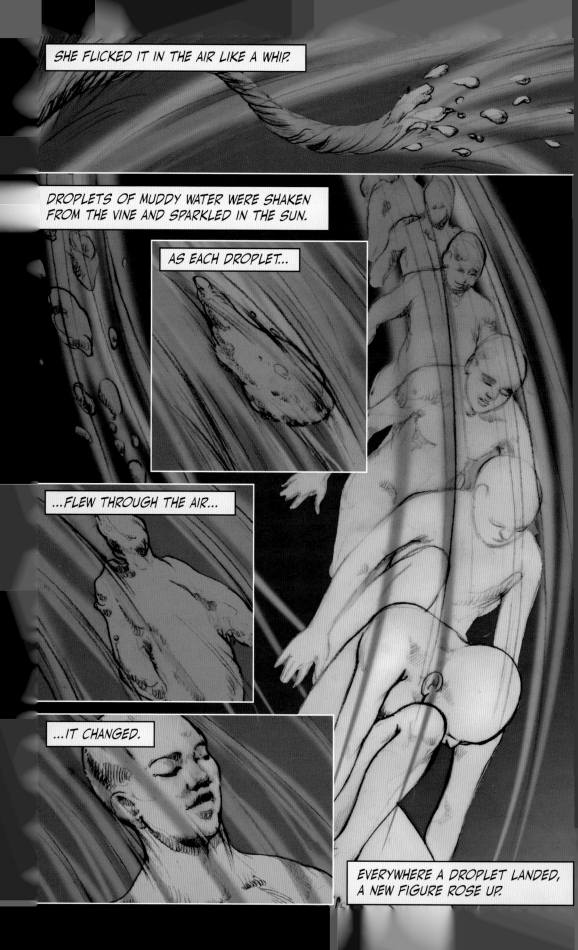

SHE FLICKED IT IN THE AIR LIKE A WHIP.

DROPLETS OF MUDDY WATER WERE SHAKEN FROM THE VINE AND SPARKLED IN THE SUN.

AS EACH DROPLET...

...FLEW THROUGH THE AIR...

...IT CHANGED.

EVERYWHERE A DROPLET LANDED, A NEW FIGURE ROSE UP.

AFTER MANY YEARS, NU WA'S FIGURES WERE LIVING ALL OVER THE WORLD. THEY HAD GROWN TALL AND STRONG. THOSE SHE HAD MADE WITH HER OWN HANDS BECAME THE RICH PEOPLE. THE ONES SPLASHED FROM THE VINE BECAME THE POOR PEOPLE.

HER WORK WAS NOT OVER. AS THE YEARS PASSED, HER PEOPLE, BOTH RICH AND POOR, WOULD GET OLD...

...AND DIE. SHE HAD TO MAKE MORE CLAY FIGURES TO REPLACE THEM.

NU WA HAD AN IDEA. SHE SCOOPED UP SOME OF THE YELLOW CLAY AND MADE TWO SPECIAL FIGURES.

THESE BECAME THE FIRST MAN AND WOMAN. PEOPLE COULD NOW HAVE FAMILIES. NU WA WOULD NOT HAVE TO DIP HER FINGERS INTO THE YELLOW CLAY AGAIN.

UNFORTUNATELY, NU WA'S WORK WAS NOT YET DONE. A WAR BETWEEN DEMONS RAGED IN THE WORLD.

IN THE DEMONS' WAR, THE FOUR GREAT PILLARS HOLDING UP THE SKY WERE SHATTERED. THEY HAD BEEN BUILT AT THE BEGINNING OF TIME, BY THE GIANT PAN GU. THEY KEPT HEAVEN AND EARTH APART. WITHOUT THEM, THE SKY AND EARTH WOULD JOIN, AND THE WORLD WOULD END.

AS THE EARTH AND THE HEAVENS STARTED TO MEET, A HOLE WAS TORN IN THE SKY, AND DARKNESS POURED THROUGH.

MOUNTAINS WERE SPLIT APART AND FIRES LEAPT FROM THE CRACKS IN THEIR SIDES.

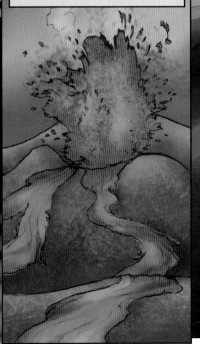

WATERS FROM DEEP BELOW THE EARTH FLOODED THE PLAINS.

WHEN NU WA SAW HOW BADLY PEOPLE WERE SUFFERING, SHE BECAME SAD. SHE KNEW SHE MUST DO SOMETHING.

FIRST, SHE PROPPED UP THE HEAVENS USING THE FOUR LEGS OF A GIANT TURTLE.

THEN, SHE SET FIRE TO BUNDLES OF REEDS.

WITH THEIR ASHES...

...SHE DAMMED THE FLOODWATERS. BUT SHE STILL HAD TO MEND THE HOLE IN THE SKY.

NU WA TOOK FIVE COLORED STONES...

...AND, USING HER POWERS, SHE MELTED THEM.

NOW DARKNESS LEFT THE WORLD. HEAVEN AND EARTH WERE APART ONCE MORE.

THE FIRES DIED DOWN, AND THE WATERS DRAINED AWAY.

NU WA SAW THAT HER PEOPLE WERE SAFE.

SHE RESTED. AND WHERE SHE LAY...

...HER SLEEPING SHAPE BECAME A VAST MOUNTAIN RANGE. NOW PEOPLE WOULD ALWAYS REMEMBER THEIR GODDESS NU WA.

THE END

THE TEN SUNS

THERE WERE ONCE TEN SUNS IN THE WORLD.

EVERY MORNING, ONE OF THE SUNS WOULD TAKE ITS TURN TO RISE IN THE EAST...

...AND TRAVEL WESTWARD ACROSS THE SKY.

COCK-A-DOODLE-DOO!

ALONG THE WAY...

...THE SUN'S FIRE WOULD GIVE WARMTH AND LIGHT TO THE LAND.

THE SUN'S JOURNEY WOULD TAKE IT TO THE FAR WEST. THERE, JUST AS THE DAY ENDED, IT WOULD DIP BEHIND MOUNT YEN-TZU AND DISAPPEAR.

IN THE WEST, BEYOND MOUNT YEN-TZU, THE SUN'S MOTHER, THE GODDESS XI HI, WOULD BE WAITING. ALL TEN OF XI HI'S CHILDREN WOULD FOLLOW HER TO THE VALLEY OF THE LIGHT IN THE EAST. THERE, SHE WOULD WASH THEM...

...AND PUT THEM TO BED IN A GIANT MULBERRY TREE CALLED FU-SANG. THEY WOULD REST IN ITS BRANCHES UNTIL IT WAS TIME FOR ANOTHER SUN TO MAKE THE JOURNEY WEST, TO MOUNT YEN-TZU.

ONE NIGHT...

AND HOW DID THE WORLD LOOK TODAY, BROTHER?

THE RIVERS SHONE LIKE SILVER SNAKES, AND THE FORESTS COVERED THE HILLS LIKE A GREEN QUILT.

I WATCHED FARMERS WORKING IN FIELDS, AND TRADESMEN BUSY IN TOWNS. I SAW EVERY LIVING THING.

IT IS A PITY I HAVE TO WAIT NINE MORE DAYS BEFORE I CAN SEE IT ALL AGAIN.

AND I HAVE FOUR DAYS TO WAIT.

I DO NOT WANT TO WAIT FOR MY TURN TO TRAVEL ACROSS THE SKY.

TOMORROW WE SHALL ALL SEE THE WORLD— TOGETHER!

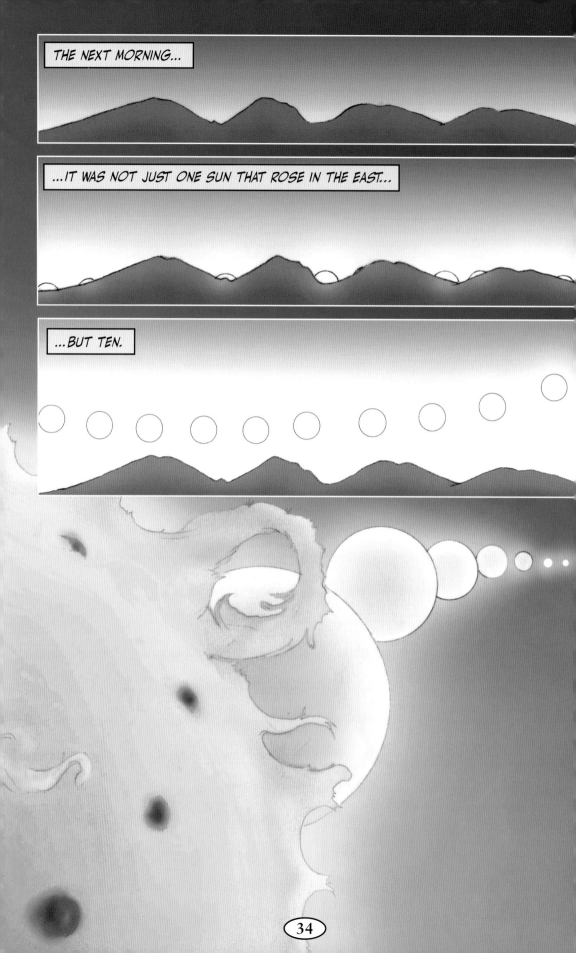

THE NEXT MORNING...

...IT WAS NOT JUST ONE SUN THAT ROSE IN THE EAST...

...BUT TEN.

THE TEN SUNS ROSE
INTO THE SKY...

...AND LOOKED DOWN.

THEY BECAME BRIGHTER...

??!!

...AND BRIGHTER.

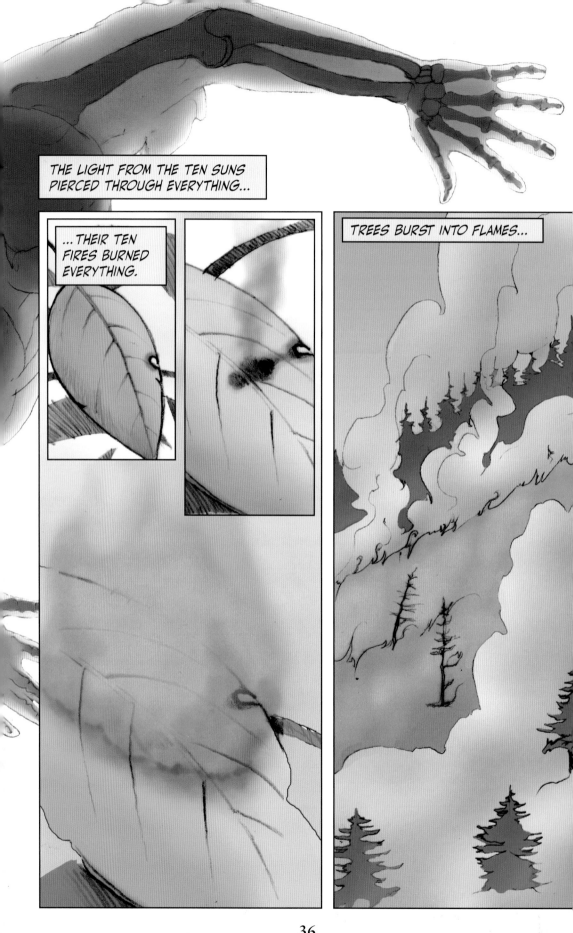

THE LIGHT FROM THE TEN SUNS PIERCED THROUGH EVERYTHING...

...THEIR TEN FIRES BURNED EVERYTHING.

TREES BURST INTO FLAMES...

...STONES ON THE GROUND MELTED...

...SEAS, RIVERS, AND LAKES BOILED AWAY...

...AND WHEREVER LIVING CREATURES TRIED TO HIDE...

...THE TEN SUNS FOUND THEM.

THE PEOPLE WERE IN DESPAIR.

WHAT CAN WE DO? WE WILL ALL DIE SOON IF THE SUNS AREN'T STOPPED.

WE MUST GO TO THE EMPEROR. HE IS GOOD AND WISE. HE WILL KNOW WHAT TO DO.

IN HIS PALACE, THE EMPEROR YAO WAS SUFFERING ALONG WITH HIS PEOPLE.

THE RIVERS HAVE DRIED UP.

OUR CROPS AND ANIMALS ARE DEAD.

VERY SOON, WE SHALL ALL BE DEAD TOO!

YOU MUST HELP US, MIGHTY LORD!

THE TEN SUNS DO NOT KNOW THE HARM THEY ARE CAUSING. I WILL SPEAK TO THEIR FATHER, DI JUN. HE MAY BE ABLE TO GET THEM TO LEAVE THE SKY.

LATER...

THEY ARE YOUR SONS, DI JUN. YOU MUST CONTROL THEM.

THEY WILL NOT LISTEN TO ME. I SHALL ASK THE IMMORTAL HERO YI TO HELP YOU.

AT DI JUN'S HOME IN THE HEAVENS...

YOU MUST NOT HARM ANY OF MY CHILDREN, YI. USE YOUR MAGIC BOW AND ARROWS TO SCARE THEM BACK TO THE VALLEY OF THE LIGHT.

YI LEFT DI JUN. HE LOOKED AROUND AT THE SCORCHED LANDS AND THEN AT THE TEN SUNS. HE LIFTED HIS MAGIC BOW AND FITTED AN ARROW.

HE TOOK AIM...

...AND FIRED.

YI DID NOT MEAN TO SCARE DI JUN'S CHILDREN...

39

...BUT TO KILL THEM!

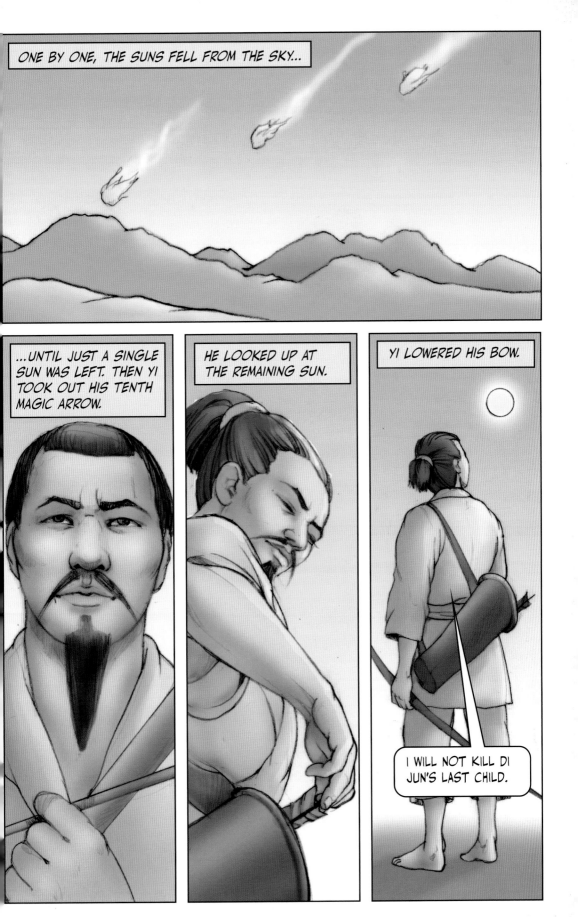

41

DI JUN WAS FURIOUS WITH YI.

YOU HAVE KILLED NINE OF MY CHILDREN! YOU MUST BE PUNISHED!

MEANWHILE, THE LAST SUN HAD SET IN THE WEST. THE NIGHTTIME BREEZES COOLED THE HOT LANDS.

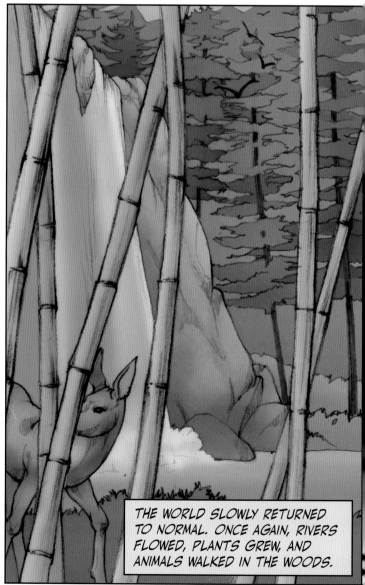

THE WORLD SLOWLY RETURNED TO NORMAL. ONCE AGAIN, RIVERS FLOWED, PLANTS GREW, AND ANIMALS WALKED IN THE WOODS.

PEOPLE WENT ON WITH THEIR DAILY LIVES.

AND FOR HIS PUNISHMENT...

...YI WAS FORCED TO LIVE ON EARTH...

...AS A MORTAL.

THE END

MORE MYTHICAL CHARACTERS

Because there are many different religious beliefs in China, there are many mythological gods, animals, and people. Here are a few of the more well-known characters.

BA SIN — These are the Eight Immortals of Daoist belief. They are eight Chinese people who lived at different times. They managed to become immortal by completing various tasks. They each look after a different thing on Earth, such as healing, music, and nature. They are symbolic of good luck in China and represent particular states in life: poverty, wealth, youth, old age, masculinity, femininity, noble people, and ordinary people.

DOU MOU — She is the goddess of the North Star, who the Daoists believe has the power to lengthen life. This is because she looks after the book of life and death. She is also known as Star Mother, and has nine children, the Jen Huang, who were the first humans to rule on Earth.

GUAN DI — He was a man who became extremely well-known as a military general in China. Hundreds of years after his death, he was made into the Chinese god of war and of martial arts. He protects China from all of its enemies. He is also the patron of literature.

GUAN YIN — A figure from Chinese Buddhism, Guan Yin is sometimes seen as a goddess and at other times as a god. A god of kindness and caring, Guan Yin looks after children in particular. Because of the charitable nature of this figure, people pray to Guan Yin when they are in difficult situations. Guan Yin can appear in many different forms.

LUNG MO — Known as the Dragon Mother, Lung Mo found a dragon's egg and raised the dragon. It brought Lung Mo and her village good luck. When she died, she was made into a goddess.

THE MEN SHEN — These are the gods of doorways. People used to paint colored pictures of these gods on their doors to keep devils away from their families. Eventually, the images of door gods were replaced by pictures of real people. Now, Men Shen are painted on houses and gates to celebrate the new year and to bring happiness.

MONKEY — A very mischievous character, Monkey was born from a stone egg. He is also known as the Great Sage, Equal of Heaven. Because he was scared of death he learned the secret of living forever. Monkey went to heaven but caused so much trouble that he was punished by Buddha. Eventually, he was sent on a quest by Guan Yin, and he finally learned how to behave himself.

PAN GU — Pan Gu created the universe. Before anything else existed, there was darkness everywhere and a huge egg, where the giant Pan Gu slept and grew bigger. Eventually, he became so big that he burst from the egg. The lighter parts of the egg, known as Yang, made the heavens, while the heavier parts, Yin, made the Earth. Pan Gu held heaven up to stop the two from coming together again. He stayed like this and grew bigger for 18,000 years. When he died, his body formed all parts of the world-the land, sea, weather, stars, moon, and humans.

TSAO WANG — A kitchen god who lives in the hearth of every household, watching the family. At the end of the year, he tells the Jade Emperor what he has seen. Then the family either has good or bad luck for the next year. Before he leaves, the family can put sweet things in his mouth so that he can say only nice things.

WEN CHANG — The Daoist god of Chinese books, literature, and writing, Wen Chang was a wise man who could predict the future. When he died, he was made into a god. He also watches over students, anybody taking exams, and all those who love books.

ZHONG KWEI — Zhong Kwei was a man who was so ugly and rejected that he decided to kill himself by drowning. Now his dreadful image is put on walls to keep away devils and evil spirits. He kills demons and eats ghosts.

GLOSSARY

apostle A firm believer in a religion.

archer A person who shoots things with a bow and arrow.

Buddhism A religion from Nepal that is based on understanding the real meaning of life rather than the worship of gods.

Confucianism A way of thinking in Chinese society taught by the philosopher, Confucius. It favors logic, education, and social values.

cosmological A type of study that looks at the stars to understand the universe–how it works and how it was formed.

culture Beliefs and customs shared by a group of people.

Daoism Now a Chinese religion, Daoism is based on magical beliefs, and was begun by the philosopher Lao-Tzu.

emperor A man who rules over a nation known as an empire.

hearth The stone floor of a fireplace.

immortality Living forever.

logical Being able to explain or do something in a clear and precise way, rather than using emotions.

mold To give shape to something by using your hands.

Mongolian A person from an ancient part of east-central Asia called Mongolia.

mortal To live for a limited amount of time. Humans are mortal.

philosopher A person who studies things using a set of ideas.

phoenix A mythological bird who lives for hundreds of years, then burns to death as it sets itself on fire, and is reborn from the ashes.

pierce To enter by force into something else.

quest A search for something.

rational To be able to look at something in a clear, calm way, rather than with emotions.

represent To stand or be a sign for an idea or an object.

sacred Something that is very important or holy.

semi mythical An event or figure that is based partly on fact and partly on the stories or myths that have developed around it.

symbolic Relating to something that holds a special meaning and is used to show this meaning to others.

unicorn A mythological creature who is very pure. The unicorn looks like a horse, but it has a single horn coming out of its forehead.

FOR MORE INFORMATION

ORGANIZATIONS

Chinese Culture Center of San Francisco
750 Kearny Street, 3rd Floor
San Francisco, CA 94108-1809
(415) 986-1822
Web site: http://www.c-c-c.org

Museum of Chinese in the Americas
70 Mulberry Street, 2nd Floor
New York, NY 10013
(212) 619-4785
Web site: http://www.moca-nyc.org

FOR FURTHER READING

Bellingham, David. *The Kingfisher Book of Mythology: Gods, Goddesses and Heroes from Around the World*. London, England: Kingfisher Publications Plc., 2001.

Dea Collier, Irene. *Chinese Mythology*. Berkeley Heights, NJ: Enslow Publishers, 2001.

Philip, Neil. *The Illustrated Book of Myths: Tales and Legends of the World*. London, England: Dorling Kindersley Limited, 1995.

Roberts, Jeremy. *Chinese Mythology A to Z*. New York, NY: Facts on File, 2004.

Sanders, Tao Tao Liu. *Dragons, Gods and Spirits from Chinese Mythology*. New York, NY: Bedrick, 1994.

Yang, Lihui. *Handbook of Chinese Mythology*. Santa Barbara, CA: ABC-CLIO, 2005.

INDEX

Web Sites

Due to the changing nature of Internet links, the Rosen Publishing Group, Inc., has developed
an online list of Web sites related to the subject of this book. This site is updated regularly.
Please use this link to access the list:
http://www.rosenlinks.com/gm/chinese